# THE CINQUE PORTS
# AND
# LORDS WARDEN

A HISTORY IN VERSE AND PROSE

*The sea shaped their history, but geography the more*
*fashioned their future, than fortune or war.*

**Poems by**
**Edward Body**

Edward Body, who by the romantic resonance of his verse and the evocative historical argot of his prose, has assembled for us, in review order, our erstwhile Cinque Ports Fleet, lining its decks with its picaresque, resourceful patriotic rogues, who, as occasion demanded, fished and ferried and fought from these shores.

Photographs by Benjamin Wood

**THE CINQUE PORTS**

HASTINGS
SANDWICH
DOVER
NEW ROMNEY
HYTHE

**THE ANTIENT TOWNS**

RYE
WINCHELSEA

**THE LIMBS**

| **Of Hastings** | **Of Sandwich** | **Of Dover** | **Of N/Romney** | **Of Rye** |
|---|---|---|---|---|
| Seaford | Fordwich | Folkestone | Lydd | Tenterden |
| Pevensey | Deal | Faversham | | |
| | Ramsgate | Margate | | |

Published by Kent Messenger and printed by Scarbutts, West Malling, England. 1992

# The Cinque Port of Dover

Roman 'Dubris' port of their coastal style,
Caesar's 'civilist place in all this isle'
Beyond the extant memory; alive
In monument, and muniment archive.

Dover, old harbour in the chalk cliff's cleft.
From whose shores Kings and armies have left.
Lone Cinque Port survivor, last to retain
Maritime greatness, command of the main.

The curse of the Port, was the eastward drift,
The piling shingle made the delta shift.
Split a river to streams; the Dour diverted,
Was sluggish and slow, sour and deserted.

It was once decreed, so chroniclers tell.
At the sound of a horn, the drift to repel;
High or low, all burgesses should mingle,
Each armed with his spade, to move the shingle!

But as you may irreverently guess.
It was something similar, more or less,
To the woman who tried to augment the sea
With a 'minikin' of water, hopefully!

Twenty-one ships, their crews and a 'grummet'
Gave to the King, at her Cinque Port summit
For fifteen days; then favours received,
No 'lastage' or 'tallage' and taxes relieved.

Same breed as of Rye and of Winchelsea
Hastings and Hythe, Sandwich with 'Romeney'
Pirates and smugglers, wreckers and rogues.
Brave men; enemies of all England's foes.

But fishermen first, whose love was the sea,
Who coaxed it, or fought it unceasingly
In boats so shaped, that sailing or rowing,
It was hard to tell which way they were going!

Fortune and disaster, vagaries of tide,
Triumph and defeat; despondency and pride.
Coastline changes, defiant of control
Gave and took away, parted and made whole.

Last sight of England, or first glimpse of home.
Haven of millions wherever they roam.
The Castle, the Straits and the Cliffs provide,
The fact and the source; and the sight of its pride.

Part of the Roman Pharos (lighthouse) still remains. Dover alone continues to be famous as a port of commerce. The Port was given royal aid in preference to the others to fight the fatal 'eastward drift' of detritus, to which they succumbed. The literal meaning of 'grummet' is a small rope ring, but it was also the name given to the boy in the crew. 'Lastage' was duty by weight, and 'tallage' duty by number. The heroic infamy of these men was known and feared by 'friend' and foe alike. The town seals show the shape of their boats, with the battle castles in position.



*Dover Harbour*

DOVER 2

# The Cinque Port of Hastings

At Hastings our England's history saw,
A battle more important than a war!
All seemed to change, after this brief affray,
From the Saxon to the Norman way.

But the Channel's the sea; William needed
These men of the Ports, to whom he ceded,
Rights and rewards, for their guile and their craft,
To watch and protect his lanes, fore and aft.

Though first of the five, from west to the east.
Each thought none greater; and none was the least!
In Brodhull and Guestling would dispute to stand,
Proudly premier, at the Speaker's right hand.

Intrepid and fierce, in the Cinque Ports style,
Its fishermen forsook their nets for a while,
To drive the Moors from the Lisbon shore.
And added a bishopric to their score!

Against Calais, and the Armada too,
And sometimes former 'friends' who hove in view,
From Yarmouth and Bruges; Ypres and Boulogne.
They were feared and avoided and left alone!

King John, while at Hastings, made a decree.
To be called 'The Ordinance of the Sea'
That ships on 'our sea' sailing upon it,
Should 'Stryke and vail their foreign bonnet'

When passing ships of his Cinque Port fleet,
On their lawful occasions, should so greet
And acknowledge these 'lords of the ocean'
With a royal salute; such was his notion.

But Black Death, silting and arson burning,
The Frenchman raiding and ever returning.
Her crews depleted, and her shipping lost.
The harbour gone — too great was the cost!

And Hastings struggled; then died as a Port.
Strangled and choked by the havoc wrought.
Victim of storm, erosion and pillage.
Became, once again, a fishing village.

From this detritus, by courage and grace,
Grew a salubrious watering place.
And as you bathe and relax here to-day,
It is hard to believe its quondam decay.

The battle of Hastings; Oct 14th 1066, was of short duration. Although not won by the English, they reaped benefits in their language, laws, culture, land ownership, architecture and building. The help of the Cinque Ports fishermen was vital to the Conqueror, but could not be forced. They agreed to co-operate if allowed to retain certain privileges. Hastings was at one time considered the premier Port, but this did not remain undisputed by the others. In 1148 its sailors helped to take Lisbon from the Moors and restore King Alphonso, so a priest of Hastings became a bishop of Lisbon. The piracy of the Portsmen was notorious, and consanguinity was no guarantee of immunity! 'Stryke and vail' etc., meant dip their topsails. The Black Death plague swept the country from 1347 to 1350, and there were French raids in 1339 and 1377. The sea inundated the harbour, but Hastings was re-born at the end of the 18th century, when sea bathing became fashionable.



*Hastings Beach*

# The Cinque Port of Hythe

You would never guess, if you didn't know,
That here the Roman Limen used to flow.
That Stutfall Castle watched the Saxon shores.
And in the sea the galleys plied their oars.

Stout and secure against human revolt,
Stutfall subsided at nature's assault.
While Limen, persuaded by Rhee, changed spate,
And, choosing Romney, left Hythe to its fate.

The men of Hythe, fearsome, brave and proud,
Rough, rugged, part of the Cinque Port crowd.
Repelled invaders, who attacked their shores,
But lived and fought to their own code of laws.

From some wrecks, that rock or storm never made,
But owed their fate to the pirates' base trade.
They took their booty; and without rancour,
Gave their Mayor the 'cable and anchor'.

Then torn by gales, and the 'eastward drift'
Black Death and the plague, and the coastline shift.
Hythe's desperate people, fearing the worst,
Threatened to leave this town, they thought accursed.

But Kingly intervention, made them stay.
He cancelled service; nor dared they disobey.
Hard though they toiled, inspired by royal urge
And fought; but lost to elemental scourge.

Now, the haven has vanished, dry the sea
At the edge of the town, where it used to be.
Only the pleasant Canal and the Towers
Remain, as reminders of anxious hours.

Superbly perched, nobly arched, and high,
Buttressed St Leonards supplicates the sky,
Perhaps all the departed souls to save,
Of those remains, in its most macabre grave!

You'd never guess, as you stand here to-day,
Watching a Venetian Fete hold sway.
Or a pageantry of Cinque Port pride
That Hythe as a town, once nearly died!

Limen was the Roman name for Rother. Stutfall was one of the Roman fortresses along the Saxon Shore which was demolished by an ancient landslip. The 'cable and anchor' were the usual 'perks' of the Warden or Mayor when salvaged from wrecks. Only the direct intervention of Henry IV prevented the burgesses from leaving Hythe, which they believed to be bewitched. The Martello Towers and the Military Canal were built by Pitt when French attacks were feared. Hundreds of skulls and bones are on display in the St Leonards crypt. The manor of Saltwood of which Hythe was a part was given to the Archbishop of Canterbury by Canute about the middle of the 14th century. Archbishop Courtenay built the present Saltwood Castle and took up residence there. He had to be continually propitiated by the burgesses of Hythe with bribes and presents! An earthquake in 1580 set the church bells ringing. In 1739 the church tower collapsed — any connection?



*Artist and Fishing Boat*

RX150

# The Cinque Port of New Romney

Centre of the Ports, and of Brodhull too.
And full of years, belies the name of 'New'
Chartered by John, and by the second Charles.
Queen Bess, who gave the 'lande betweene the walles'

'A hideous tempest, threw down steeples'
Affrighted brave men, and killed its peoples.
Struck their town, and its flood and recession.
Smashed ships, houses and precious possession.

Their living threatened by an 'act of God'
Undismayed, they dug his church from the mud.
Then dragged the plough through the bed of the sea.
Now pasture their sheep, where it used to be.

Gone now, are Rother's mouth and Romney Bay.
Where spindrift waves once splashed in spume-flecked spray.
Rich sea-bed pasture nourishes the flock.
The best of breeds, like all of Romney stock!

Romney, when raided, pillaged stormed and burned
Reciprocal upon the raider turned.
But when they engaged in the 'moonlit trade'
These very foes, as friends would masquerade.

Gone now the 'owlers' since more 'lookers' came.
For sheep, not ships or brandy make her name.
Marshmen and Portsmen, at peace, side-by-side
In landlocked amity, at last abide!

But not without strife of a bitter sort,
Before Romney lost its worth as a Port,
Did these rival factions at last find peace.
In the common bond of the 'Golden Fleece'?

In the grey owl-light of approaching night,
Silhouettes change colour to black and white.
And Marsh mists rise a foot clear of the ground,
And all around the Marsh frog's mating sound.

How easy then, to forget that it's now,
To allow your thoughts to slip back somehow,
To strain your ears for the 'owler's' call.
And wonder at the vastness of it all.

Changed, but dignified in diminution,
Proud of pageant and of constitution.
To 'lie and live' under the pleasant yoke.
Is the happy choice of Romney folk.

New Romney is the centre of the five Cinque Ports and two Antient Towns. It was traditionally the meeting place of the Brotherhood, known as the 'Brodhull' and was the Portsmen's own court. A charter was granted by King John, and by Elizabeth I in 1563. 'Lande betweene the walles' is the silted-up channel of the Rhee wall. Several feet of detritus had to be dug out of the church after the storm of 1287, which also diverted the river Rother towards Rye. French raids on Romney were returned by raids on France, but this did not stop the exchange of fleeces for spirits. 'Moonlight trade' is smuggling, and 'lookers' are shepherds. 'Owlers' are smugglers. 'Golden Fleece' are Romney Marsh sheep.



*Dymchurch to Hythe small gauge Railway*

# The Cinque Port of Sandwich

Old Sandwich, a stade for the crossing of Kings.
Attacked by the Danes in their foragings.
Hard by the Romans Richborough fort.
A Domesday 'hundred' a famous Cinque Port.

Pledged to provide in those troubled days
A score of ships, and their crews to raise.
Given 'honours at Court' and 'den and strond'
By royal favour, for keeping this bond.

Stepping aboard, or walking ashore.
Princes and prelates were there by the score.
And once the triumphant'sable heir'
Brought as prisoner, John of Poitiers.

Sandwich streets, where houses strain to touch,
Customs not changed by time overmuch.
When St Peter's 'pig bell' tolled at eight,
Now ghosts within the silent shadows wait.

From here Becket left these shores for a while.
Banished by Henry to lonely exile.
Landed at Gravelines; then restored to glory.
Returned to Sandwich 'Vado in Angliam Mori'.

Alone in sober sable garbs its Mayor,
Still mourns the victim of a foreign slayer.
Protects him with a new-cut blackthorn switch,
From the evils of an imagined witch!

St Bartholomew's Day lives on in history,
A Hospice name, a battle and a victory.
At Sandwich haven by the Goodwin Bank
De Burgh with some lime, the Frenchman sank!

Beset by attack, her buildings burned,
By her endurance her survival was earned.
With grace and charity, her aid extended
To Dutch and Walloon, whom she befriended.

For their devotions gave to them a shrine,
Dutch cupola'd St Peters, a gift benign.
The 'gentle strangers' with their skills replied,
And saved a Port, deserted by its tide.

But can any past catastrophe match
The awful violation of this quiet patch
By the incessant, vibrant traffic roar
That shakes its history, from roof to floor?

Sandwich was once the most famous Port. 'Stade' means landing place. It was raided by the Danes up to the early 11th century. 'Honours at Court' was the right to bear the canopy over the Sovereign at the Coronation. 'Sable heir' refers to the Black Prince; his prisoner, King John of France. The 'pig bell' was the signal for pigs to be let out to scavenge the streets! The Mayor wears black in memory of a predecessor murdered by the French. Each new Mayor receives a blackthorn switch. Hubert de Burgh caused lime to be thrown into the faces of the boarding enemy. Sandwich was repeatedly raided and razed by the French. Queen Elizabeth persuaded the Port to accept Dutch and Walloon refugees, who taught their hosts market gardening and weaving. Becket left here for a six year exile in 1164 and on returning is said to have remarked, 'I go into England to die'.



*View from the Swing Bridge*

# The Antient Town of Rye

Rye gained Rother, when by storm oppressed,
Romney was of Rother dispossessed.
Rye from fire and ash by the French arose.
As a sanctuary for the Huguenots

Rye monastic, was once to Fecamp tied.
Ceded by Canute; a promise ratified.
Rye the 'foreign' most cruelly miscalled.
But dubbed 'Rye Royal' by a Queen enthralled.

Rye an Antient Town, paired with Winchelsea.
Pledged ships and service, if need be,
Sailors, fierce unscrupulous and brave,
Smugglers, fishermen and many a knave!

From Gun Garden round to Watchbell Green,
Their eyes once scanned a different scene
Than now before us calm and pleasant lies;
For foe or storm could take them by surprise.

Rye nepotic; in thrall to a civic clique.
Her two maces, a privilege unique.
Rye, safe haven for a stranded King,
A chance godfather at a christening!

Rye the maritime and Rye the rural,
Varied, picturesque, a moving mural.
Here and there a stretch of 'bouldered' street,
Pleasing to the eye, hard upon the feet!

Rye quiet and quaint, with a Flemish air,
History combined with a modern flair.
Young for its age, with a sense of the past.
Blended and separate, but neither outclassed.

Highest of all, her crowning glory stands,
Risen from its ruins at the Frenchman's hands.
Cartouche and Clock and Quarter Boys look down
From St Mary's tower above the town.

Memories now, are Postern, Baddings, Strand.
Extant, as reminders, Ypres and the Land.
The Mint, the Quay, Lamb House and Cinque Port Street,
Evoke past greatness; the picture is complete.

The first two lines refer to the storm of 1287 which changed the course of the river Rother. Rye was sacked and burned by the French in 1377, and in the 17th century gave sanctuary to the Huguenots. It stands on three rivers, the Rother, the Tillingham and the Brede. There were four gates in the town wall, called Land, Baddings, Strand and Postern, of which only Land remains. Rye was given by Canute to the Abbey of Fecamp, hence the term 'Rye the foreign' but was repossessed by Henry III. 'Rye nepotic' refers to the fact that in over 100 years all but ten of the Mayors were from four inter-related families pledged to nominate each other! The Bailiff and the Mayor each had a mace, and when the two offices were merged, the maces were retained by the Mayor. King George I, blown ashore in a storm, took refuge in the Mayor's house, and stood Godfather to his son. The church is named St Mary the virgin.

# The Antient Town of Winchelsea

You'll feel the enchantment, as you advance
On Coventry Patmore's 'town in a trance'
His 'sunny dream of centuries ago'
More of its history, you'll want to know.

Drowned without trace by a twice flowing tide.
All lost, but the fiery spur of its pride.
Renewed from the flood; as Rye from the flame.
Ditched, walled and gated, and proud of its name.

Far seeing triumph of a royal plan,
Before the old submerged, the new began.
Built high on lofty Iham's splendid view,
Its nine and thirty chessboard quarters grew.

Plagued by pestilence, fire, sword and the sea.
Blessed now by peace and sweet tranquillity.
Once betrayed and beaten, destroyed, laid waste.
It survived and prospered; a town replaced.

Fierce as the storm, salt as the flying spray.
Old Winchelsea nurtured her men that way.
In times of peace, or when there was war,
They fished and ferried and fought from this shore.

'Antient Town' contiguous to Rye,
Greater once, then lesser, rival and ally.
Linked by history; each deprived by fate.
Enriched by time, to charm and fascinate.

Now, gently detached, untouched and remote.
Nor crowded with sails, or vessels afloat,
Not a keg or a vat brought in for a fleece.
Nor a raid to disturb its well-earned peace.

St Thomas the Martyr, splendid, alone.
Anderida's wood and Normandy's stone.
Weathered and worn; its old chancel a nave.
Traces of transepts and of stone architrave.

Drink at St Leonards, and you'll leave your heart,
In its safe keeping; for though you depart
'Tis said you'll come back to claim what you own.
Then stay there for ever, and make it home!

Coventry Patmore, the English poet, lived 1823–1896. Old Winchelsea was partly submerged in 1250 and again in 1287. The town was re-sited and re-built on Iham to a plan by Edward I, and divided into 39 areas or quarters with the streets at right angles. Winchelsea suffered by the plague and French raids, and was betrayed by a citizen who admitted the French by the Town Gate. The fortunes of Rye and Winchelsea alternated with geographical changes. The real name of the church is St Thomas of Canterbury. It is built of Sussex oak and Caen stone, and is partly ruin, with the old transepts gone and the chancel used as a nave. St Leonards is a well by the old windmill, and there is a legend which says that if you drink of its waters, you will go back to Winchelsea.



*Winchelsea Church*

# The Limb of Deal

The cliffs of Dover were bristling with spears
When Caesar came, and so great were his fears,
That he sailed on to seek flatter regions.
Less dangerous for landing his Roman legions.

He followed the coastline into the Downs,
To the shore of Deal, towards Thanet's towns.
And landing here he conquered the Briton,
Thus was a passage of history written.

He took some hostages and sailed away.
Came back with more legions, this time to stay.
Roman coins have since been found.
In places where hills and barrows abound.

Deal on her arms notes that Roman invasion.
The left supporter marks the occasion,
A Roman soldier, who first leaped ashore.
And on the right, a Marine of the Corps.

Below the beguiling shallows of the sea.
Lurk the Goodwin Sands; unseen treachery.
While between the shore and those fatal mounds
The safe anchorage of the deeper Downs.

Were these same Goodwins, once Godwin's land
A fertile island, now covered with sand?
History and legend cannot agree,
About this mound which is under the sea.

It was from the Downs that the Cinque Ports fleet,
Of forty ships sailed bravely to meet
The eighty French, who appeared at the time.
And conquered them with the aid of some lime!

The men of Deal put humanity first.
'Adjuvate Advenus' let the storms do their worst.
Lodemanage pilots, hovellers of wrecks.
Who knew Goodwin's menace; her fatal effects.

This Sandwich Limb with the uniform shore.
For rescue and succour, still to the fore.
Among those of the sea, may justly claim,
A place with their Port in Cinque Port fame.

Although now, not all are men of the sea.
Time has not changed them essentially.
True to their motto, they welcome the stranger,
Are generous in need, steadfast in danger.

Caesar twice landed in Deal, in 55BC and 54BC. Deal's Arms were granted in 1968, and include the Lord Warden's Oar. 'Supporters' are the figures on either side of the escutcheon. The Roman soldier alludes to the invasion of 55/54BC. The Marines have long been associated with Deal. Legend has it that the Goodwin Sands were once part of Earl Godwin's lands, which became submerged. When one thinks of Winchelsea, this is not impossible! In 1217 the fleet defeated superior French forces, partly by throwing lime into the faces of the boarding parties (see also Sandwich) The Court of Lodemanage was set up in the reign of Henry VIII to regulate pilotage affairs. Hovellers were unlicensed pilots, and salvagers of wrecks. Deal lifeboatmen were famous for their bravery.
The Deal Coat of Arms bears the motto 'Adjuvate Advenus' Befriend the Stranger.



*Ball and Shaft on Timeball Tower which was connected electrically to Greenwich for sailors at sea to set their chronometers*

BEAU JESSE
DEAL
SUMALLEY

# The Limb of Faversham

It's hard to believe, as you wend your way,
Through Faversham's streets, in the present day
That Saxons and Romans once settled here,
And near the town died Queen Boadicea.

Athelstan enacted property laws,
And levied tithes in the monastic cause.
Churches were from taxes, by Wihtred freed.
And the Abbots thrived in unholy greed.

Here Crispin was said to have followed his trade,
Cobbling and stitching the shoes that he made.
And the barons fought the church's power.
Imprisoned the Abbot in Dover's tower.

In the year twelve-hundred and twenty-nine,
Shipping ordinance a part did assign,
To Faversham folk, in England's defence.
With Cinque Port privilege as recompense.

Chartered to Dover; a Limb of that Port,
By their side the men of Faversham fought,
And one, Henry Pay, commanded the fleet.
That took six score ships, and cargoes complete.

A grateful fifth Henry, with royal grace,
Fixed the Cinque Port arms to Faversham's mace.
Attached to its head, so that all might see,
And carried with pride in the Liberty.

In the shipyards and wharves by the Swale,
Faversham fashioned its ships and its sail.
And in the quays and the hides of the Creek
'Owlers' and Revenue, played hide and seek!

Faversham captured its fugitive Lord,
Afloat in a hoy, with courtiers aboard.
The second James caught, escaping to France.
Was most displeased at this grievous mischance!

His Majesty was then most quickly interned.
These men, with his rank, were not much concerned.
And, making it infinitely worse,
Three hundred guineas, they stole from his purse!

But time and tide; most especially tide.
The limited efforts of man defied.
It silted the Ports and altered the shore.
Till harbours and havens existed no more.

Legend has it, that Boadicea took poison after defeat and died near Faversham. Athelstan, circa 924, held a court here to levy tithes. Wihtred King of Kent exempted the church from taxes. The C.P. fleet, in 1405 captured 120 French ships with cargoes of iron, salt and wine. 'Owlers' see N/Romney. James II was captured by local fishermen as he tried to escape to France and suffered indignities at their hands. A 'hoy' was a small vessel for carrying goods or passengers. The eastward drift of sand and shingle gradually blocked the Ports and Limbs. St Crispin is the patron saint of leatherworkers. The barons and the church were in conflict, and in this instance Geoffrey de Bocton, the Abbot trespassed on Port jurisdiction. The Mayor arrested and held him in Dover Castle, whereupon the Archbishop excommunicated the Warden!



*Peter Alexander Smith: Beachcomber*
*Well-known local character*

# The Limb of Folkestone

Half encircled by the hills which lie,
In graceful contoured curves against the sky.
Are views of beauty, rural and marine.
While the Folkestone Leas make a charming scene.

Known to the Romans, who left their traces,
Coins and relics; foundations of places.
And other treasures dug up from the ground,
In the East Cliff area, have since been found.

Here, Eanswythe's nunnery was England's first,
But both Danes and tides have done their worst,
Despoiled and destroyed in savage assault,
This christian edifice, from roof to vault.

Inroaded and worn by the probing sea.
Pillaged and burned in spiteful villainy,
By Godwin the exile; a vengeful raid.
While traitors and Frenchmen on Folkestone preyed.

Once taxed to provide for powder and shot.
Folkestone responded with 'scot and lot'
To arm and equip the Cinque Port fleet.
A threatened second invasion to meet.

Ordered to provide one ship and her crew.
To aid the Head Port the French to pursue.
Linked with Dover in the Cinque Port elite.
With her in many a maritime feat.

Head Port and Limb did not always agree,
Over findals and wreck, and toll of the sea.
And sometimes rough internecine strife,
Sabotaged the pattern of Cinque Port life!

St Mary's and Eanswythe's church on the Bayle,
Lost two arches by the force of a gale.
Bereft of its Priory, now stands alone.
Has its patron's bones in a wall of stone.

At the churchyard cross; if you had been there.
You'd have seen the people making their Mayor,
Receiving sixpence for putting their mark
When the roll had been called by the Town Clerk.

The town does not forget her famous son.
(Nor should the world, for what he has done)
They have erected his statue to stand,
Hand on his heart; and a heart in his hand!

Roman foundations were excavated at Eastcliff. The nunnery of St Eanswythė, the daughter of Eadbald, King of Kent, was the first to be built in England. Earl Godwin, outlawed by Edward the Confessor, ravaged the coast of Kent in revenge in 1052. 'Scot and lot' was the term used in the Middle Ages for a share of tax paid by persons in chartered towns. In December 1705 two of the church arches were blown down by violent winds; only one was rebuilt which shortened the church. William Harvey, physician to James and Charles I, and the discoverer of the circulation of the blood was born in Folkestone. The statue on the famous Leas depicts him holding his right hand over his heart, and in his extended left hand is a model of a heart.
A replica of this statue has been placed outside the modern hospital which bears his name.



*William Harvey discovered blood circulation in 1628*
*(Picture by courtesy of the Kent Messenger)*

HARVEY
HOTEL

# The Limb of Fordwich

This pastoral hamlet, and watered nook.
By the silted Stour, has a sleepy look,
Quiet and quaint, with little to show,
Of its vigorous life of long ago.

Then, it was Canterbury's harbour and port.
Where ships Caen stone for the edifice brought.
A borough too, with Corporation and Mayor.
Had a Merchant Guild; an honour most rare.

Famous for fishermen, and for their fish.
Its trout fulfilled every epicure's wish.
There's a fisherman's tale that goes the rounds
That one was caught, weighing twenty-eight pounds!

Fordwich Mayor's Arms have a lion and fish,
The lion passant, and the fish on a dish.
Of this there can be no shadow of doubt
That the fish on a dish is a trout!

Here, wrangled a greedy Abbot and Prior,
Over landing tolls, quay, and of warehouse hire.
One built, one destroyed, in anger or spite.
And each invoked God, to prove he was right!

The small Town Hall, where justice was meted.
Scarcely room for a jury when seated.
A sentence passed here, was just as severe,
As savage Custumal dispensed anywhere.

Always desirous of river and creek,
To strengthen their claim, or increase their clique.
The Cinque Ports annexed this port on the Stour.
A Sandwich 'Limb' to augment her power.

Not noted as others for sea and ships,
The Fordwich haven was soon in eclipse.
But continued 'dues' and gave her support,
With 'ship money' to the purse of her Port.

A lovely hamlet in a sheltered nook.
But once more a town in the civic book.
Service and history have gained reward,
For this Sandwich 'Limb' so long ignored.

So, sit by the bridge, as you ruminate,
How mortal the famous, little the great.
And as you study the trout in the Stour
Reflect that they also, have had their hour!

The edifice is of course, Canterbury Cathedral, and the Caen stone used for its construction was brought up the Stour to Fordwich. The town was the only Merchant Guild in the Confederation, and famous in medieval times for the size and quality of its trout. There were quarrels between the Abbot of St Augustines and the Prior of Christchurch over the right to use the port. The Abbot twice demolished buildings erected by the Prior! The particular capital punishment laid down in the Fordwich Custumal (local laws) was that the prosecutor should be the executioner, and drown the guilty party, who was bound with his hands behind his bent knees, from a special place called 'thefeswelle'. Eventually the silting of the river reduced its navigability and the town lost its usefulness and importance. Fordwich, however, has successfully taken advantage of new laws, which enable parishes 'with an appropriate evidence of suitability' to claim Town Council designation.



*Fordwich Church and River*

# The Limb of Lydd

As you look towards Lydd, from miles around,
You see, rising heavenward from the ground
The church of All Saints, an impressive sight.
Four pinnacles mark the top of its height.

The tower is tall, and the Marsh is flat,
But, even making allowance for that,
This 'Marsh Cathedral' a majestic place,
For size and beauty, a city would grace.

Given by Offa into Canterbury's care.
Lydd was an island, when the Danes sailed there.
For a branch of the Limen flowed between
The Port of Romney, and its Lydd demesne.

A vista most vast; acres of shingle.
Where man and marine ecology mingle.
Even under the town and the lush green grass,
Detritus of pebble and shingle, mass.

Romney's Limb in the Cinque Port alliance,
One ship of five, to share her compliance.
An accomplice too, in the 'moonlit trade'
And with her in many a coastal raid.

Of old, chartered by a succession of Kings.
Aided by 'Advocants' buying these things.
The 'Archbishop's men' claimed findals and wreck,
With only Brodhull to hold them in check.

Here, Caxton, the Custumal on vellum wrote,
Of crime and punishment; numerous quote
Of law and order, or reward and right.
Little of pardon, but much to indite!

So time passes, and now 'lookers' and sheep,
Have taken the place of 'owlers' and 'creep'
Those men of the sea, now men of the land.
Stranded, without ships and contraband.

But with a history of valour; their fame
Though shadowed at times with piracy's shame,
Is cherished in archive, record and file.
Re-lived in pageantry, once in a while.

Now little that's nautical seems to exist,
Since sea became land by nature's twist.
And yet in Lydd folk there still seems to be
This inherited, inborn love of the sea.

The tower of All Saints is 132 feet high, and the church is known in Kent as 'The Cathedral of the Marsh!" In 774 Lydd was given to the See of Canterbury by Offa, King of Mercia, who conquered Kent. Limen was the old name for the river Rother. The whole town is built on shingle. Romney had to supply five ships to the Cinque Port fleet, of which one was from Lydd. The 'moonlit trade' is smuggling. 'Lookers' are shepherds, 'owlers' are smugglers, and a 'creep' is an iron device used by smugglers. 'Archbishop's men' were so called because their overlord was the Archbishop of Canterbury. Brodhull was the Portsmen's own Court. 'Advocants' were persons who, by paying annual subscriptions to the Ports could partake of some of their privileges. Thomas Caxton was the Town Clerk of Lydd. The 'Custumal' was the code of laws.

ROMNEY MARSH IN
WAR + PEACE
designed and painted by Simon, Miriam + members of the youth set....
SPONSERED BY ROMNEY MARSH ARTS FESTIVAL

# The Limb of Margate

A Cinque Port 'Limb' united with Dover.
Came to her aid, when the French came over.
Joined the siege of Calais, with fifteen craft.
Always in the van, and never abaft!

From Woodchurch, Goresend, and St Johns they came.
But as men of Margate; one and the same.
The beacon light told the French were in sight,
To be fought and beaten, by Cinque Port might.

By riot and fire, town records were lost,
And history now is paying the cost.
John Ball fanned the flame the poll tax created,
When buildings were burned, and archives cremated.

Dutch William and Mary used to commute,
From Margate to Holland; their usual route.
And the Elector Palatine left this shore.
Involving us in The Thirty Years War.

Marlborough left here, to join with Eugene,
To fight in battles after Blenheim.
Returning in triumph after the wars.
Honoured by England, for saving her cause.

Her Irish mace bears the name of Kinsale.
Her Arms, gules and azure; a shield per pale.
Chevron, horse rampant, demi-lion and hull.
First to be granted to Margate in full.

As well a ships and objects marine,
Margate produced the bathing machine.
In Beale's wheeled box, ladies shed their clothes.
Emerged wearing others; with criss-crossed hose!

The people of London used to enjoy
Adventurous trips on a Margate 'hoy'
Then later, when trains took over from sail,
Went faster, but more sedately by rail.

'Meregate' a break in the cliffs to the sea.
With 'Romansgate' sharing prosperity.
These Thanet towns, inseparably paired
By trials and triumphs, mutually shared.

One with Dover; one with Sandwich aligned.
They were, in history, both of one kind,
As villages, towns, and Limbs of Ports
Now sharing fame as pleasant resorts.

Margate was mentioned as a member of Dover in the King's Ordinance of Shipping in 1229. The siege of Calais was in 1347. There were serious riots in Kent in 1381 and the poll tax was thought to be one of the causes. This tax was paid by every person over fifteen. The inflammatory preaching of John Ball, the 'mad priest' helped the rising. Town records were burnt to increase the difficulty of collecting. 'Dutch William' was William III, the stadholder of Holland, who succeeded James II. The Elector was the son-in-law of James I on whose behalf England was dragged into The Thirty Years War. Eugene was an Italian prince and Austrian soldier. Refused entry into the French Army, he fought against them with Marlborough. The mace belonged to Kinsale in Ireland, and was presented to Margate in 1865. Margate's Arms were the first to be granted (as opposed to confirmed) in the Confederation in 1858. 'Gules' means red, and 'per pale' divided down the middle. The bathing machine was invented by Benjamin Beale. Romansgate is Ramsgate.



*Margate Beach*

# The Limb of Pevensey

Once called 'Anderida' a Roman name.
Then a nepotic gift to Robert Mortain,
Who built his castle by the Roman fort,
To hold and defend this 'Limb' of a Port.

But Anderida is a port no more,
Now a mile of land from its quondam shore.
For the drifting sand left Pevensey,
With alluvial land as her boundary.

Treasures and relics, now reward man's toil.
Cunobeline's coins came up with the spoil,
And the bones of a Celtic ox were found.
With some Roman cordage, from this ground.

The Conqueror stepped ashore and stumbled,
Regarded his hands; and in them crumbled
The soil of Pevensey, was greatly pleased,
And remarked that he had his kingdom seized!

Here, by an event on a single day,
This island's way of life was swept away.
When the Norman stepped on the Saxon shore,
And then at Hastings, won a day long war.

And Stamford too far from Pevensey was,
For the luckless Harold and all because
Of Hardrada and father Godwin's kin.
The defenceless shore let the Norman in.

Heroes and victims of reprisal and raid,
For the battles fought, and the forays made.
The Pevensey folk now walk where they sailed.
When the sea receded; a livelihood failed.

This historic site had a street of flint,
Possessed at one time a Norman Mint,
A Courthouse, Mayor and Corporation.
Was a Limb in the Confederation.

Sharing with others in this community,
Privileged practice and rare immunity.
Too precious, and too strong to be punished.
At most, gently reproved or admonished.

Not much recorded in script or on stone.
Obscure and forgotten, now all alone.
To-day what we are, we never would be,
Had William not landed at Pevensey!

William gave Pevensey to William Mortain, his half-brother, Roman findings were excavated near the well of the outer fort. Cymbeline (or Cunobeline) circa AD 43 was the King of the Britons. It is said that the Conqueror fell down at Pevensey, to the alarm of his followers, who regarded it as an ill omen; not so William who turned it to advantage! Harold was fighting his own brother Tostig at Stamford Bridge at the time and could not reach Pevensey to oppose the landing.
Because of their value to the King as his only marine force, the Ports and their Limbs could 'getaway with murder' and frequently did! They were his navy, but on their terms!



*Pevensey Castle (Norman)*

# The Limb of Ramsgate

The Port of Ramsgate with the golden sands,
Has Smeaton's harbour, where the obelisk stands.
Within the arm of the sheltering pier.
Close to the Downs and the anchorage there.

A 'ville' of Sandwich, and a Cinque Port 'Limb'
A mariners' berth in the interim,
Levying her 'droits' and 'foying' the Downs.
Lies south of a cordon of Thanet towns.

Ten thousand men bade England adieu.
Left Ramsgate to fight and win Waterloo.
Thousands later, blessed the sight of its shore,
A temporary respite from Hitler's war.

The front line of action; it bore the brunt,
In two world wars, on the Thanet front.
Gave succour and aid, in rescue and care.
'Salus Aegris' Ramsgate people were there.

No storm could hold back the Ramsgate boat,
While there was hope that the wreck was afloat
And its crew in peril; ignoring their own,
'Salus Naufragus' they fought it alone.

Ramsgate used its church in the normal way,
To marry and christen, bury and pray.
But when, in the wars, the bombs rained down,
Its crypt gave shelter to the folk of the town.

The Dunkirk window emblazons the time,
When courage and valour touched the sublime.
With people like this, no cause could be lost.
So enemies found to their ultimate cost!

Ramsgate's Arms tell its tale, quartered and crossed.
Rescue and safety, whatever the cost.
The lion, the ship, the dolphin and horse
With men of the lifeboat and coastguard of course!

But 'Romansgate' is old, without a doubt.
Long by the shadow of Sandwich kept out,
And by Stonar too, it may be supposed.
Till the misfortunes of one, the other transposed.

The present harbour was built in the 18th century under the direction of John Smeaton, of Eddystone fame. The obelisk commemorates the use of the Port by George IV, when visiting Hanover. He conferred the title of 'Royal' on the harbour. 'Droits' were harbour dues, and 'foying' was the profitable business of conveying stores etc., to ships harboured in the Downs. The 'little ships' of Ramsgate, including the lifeboat, formed part of the rescue flotilla at Dunkirk. The Motto 'Salus Naufragus' 'Salus Aegris' is on the town Coat of Arms, a broad translation being Safety of the shipwrecked, Safety of the sick. The lifeboatman and coastguard are the 'Supporters' on the left and right of the escutcheon. The epic of Dunkirk is commemorated by a stained glass window in the church. Stonar was an ancient Port on the Wantsum, whose decline helped Ramsgate to achieve importance as a Port. Romansgate is an old name for Ramsgate.



*Fisherman on the Pier*

# The Limb of Seaford

The Conqueror's gift to William Warenne.
Among towns and manors he gave to his men.
When he shared out England among his knights.
With its thegns, villeins, and agrarian rights.

A blend of Downland, the shore and the sea,
Once a corporate Port in its history.
A Hastings 'Limb' in a cordon of Ports.
With charters and rights to hold their own courts.

Their misleading lights hung out at night
The cause of many a foreigner's plight.
In their zeal for cargo, findal and wreck.
With never a law to hold them in check!

But no wreck, if man or beast were alive.
So, to make it so, they would contrive
To be predatory pirates, tardy to aid,
Cynically patient, in a sinister trade!

But, nevertheless, as the years progress.
The good seems greater, the infamy less
For they fought England's foes, espoused her cause.
Hated her enemies, and guarded her shores.

When nature upon herself made war.
The Ouse burst its banks, moving the shore
Away to the west; to Meeching diverted.
So Newhaven was born, from Seaford deserted.

Here, nature's fierce and turbulent forces,
Smashed and battered man's feeble resources,
The chronicler tells, and it must be right,
That towns drowned, and rivers moved in a night.

Here, stands the last, most westerly tower,
Of Pitt's defensive seventy-four.
Along the wide open, invasion coast.
Facing the foe that England feared most.

Now Seaford, once a corporate Port,
Has become a bracing sea-side resort.
With sea front walks, and paths over the Downs.
Among the most charming of Sussex towns.

By their charters, all wrecks along their coast became their property; but if man or beast escaped alive, the wreck did not belong to the Portsmen. If wrecks did not occur often enough they were helped to happen! In the reign of Henry VIII, Sir Nicholas Pelham trapped and defeated the French under their High Admiral at Seaford. In the storm of 1579 the river Ouse flooded at Meeching and cut into the sea; so Meeching was re-named Newhaven. The last of Pitt's Martello Towers along the Kent and Sussex coastline, built as defences against possible invasion, and said to number seventy-four, was at Seaford.



*Boat and Winch*

# The Limb of Tenterden

Deep in the forest of Andredsweald,
Through an open clearing, perhaps a field.
There was made, in the days of the Saxon thegn,
Between the dwellings, a long straight lane.

The grass still grows in the busy street.
But along its sides, all trimmed and neat,
Green-margined, pleasantly broad and straight,
From the old Town Pound, to Heronden's gate.

Of old St Mildred's church indited stands,
Of allegedly drowning the Goodwin Sands.
And of the slow decline of Sandwich Bay.
When the Abbot diverted its stone away.

On this church tower, in an iron kettle,
Burned resin and coal, to call to battle,
The Cinque Port folk, when the Armada came.
And a hundred parishes saw its flame.

When asked by Rye to augment her forces.
She came to her aid with men and horses.
So a corporate precedent was wrought.
When a Kentish 'Limb' succoured a Sussex Port!

'Quit of shire and hundred' and 'lovecope free'
'Rivage and ponsage' and toll of the sea,
Its Smallhythe haven, now dried and remote,
Once rivalled others, with vessels afloat.

Like Sandwich and Rye, in her charity too,
From compassion, fame and industry grew.
The trade of wool, from the Fleming learned,
Who, in distress, had to Tenterden turned.

A rural centre of the Wealden scene.
Placid, unhurried, this Saxon 'dene'
Though enterprise grows, it will not consume,
Nor ambition darken, but only illume.

Go out of your way, to go there one day,
So that when asked, you can truthfully say,
That now you know what the chronicler meant.
When he spoke of those folk of Wealden Kent.

The whole district was once a huge forest known to the Romans as Silva Anderida, and to the Saxons as Andredsweald. The story goes that the Abbot who was the overlord, used Bethersden stone intended for the sea defence of Sandwich to build the tower of St Mildred's church. It is said that a hundred churches can be seen from its summit. The town was a corporate of the Cinque Ports, and attached to Rye.
'Quit of shire and hundred' means among other things, having its own courts. 'Lovecope free' means free of taxes and tolls. 'Rivage' is landing duty, and 'Ponsage' a bridge toll. Refugee Flemings were encouraged to settle in Tenterden and taught the inhabitants woolcraft and weaving.



*Tenterden High Street*

# Three Wardens at Walmer

Walmer Castle, once an eighth Henry's fort.
'Mutatis mutandis' was made a resort,
For thrice Warden Sackville; that youthful pawn,
Raised and deposed, praised and forsworn.

Dover's cliffs confront 'les falaises blanches'
In smiling amity across 'la Manche'
But anxious eyes, once watched the strip between,
From Walmer's ramparts, Pitt surveyed the scene.

Pitt feared the French; and so great his fears,
He formed his 'Fencibles' and Volunteers.
Became their colonel, used his Warden's powers
To dig a canal, and build his towers.

Foresight or folly, who now can tell,
Did they deter, or defer, would they repel?
Hindsight or history can never be sure.
One thing is certain; unassailed they endure.

A rigid realist, austere and spare of speech,
Wellington walked on Walmer's pebbled beach.
Approved the Castle's solid rounded towers.
Enjoyed the shade of Stanhope's leafy bowers.

He may have gazed from Walmer's level coast,
Toward Ramsgate, where he embarked his host
Those years before, to win at Waterloo,
And England's ancient enemy subdue.

Peacefully at Walmer, he breathed his last,
A tranquil end; quietly he passed
Through the dark and lonely portal,
The way of great and small, in all that's mortal.

Early in the 18th century, Walmer Castle was made the official residence of the Lord Warden of the Cinque Ports. The first recorded user was Lionel Sackville, Duke of Dorset, who lived at nearby Knole House, and much of the original conversion from fort to residence must have been done for him, or by him. Some Wardens appear to have used it as a kind of holiday home, some not at all, while others have added considerably to its amenities and charm, and have lived there for relatively short periods. In general, however, it is not now much used as a residence, and is open to the public. Lady Hester Stanhope, Pitt's niece and housekeeper was mainly responsible for the layout of the gardens. William Pitt took a great interest in the building of a long and defensive Military Canal, and the construction of more than seventy Martello Towers along the coast, as far to the west as Seaford, to repel possible French attacks, which, however, never materialised. Fencibles were a kind of Home Guard! Martello Towers were named after a tower on Cape Martello, Corsica, which a British squadron had found to be impregnable. (1794)